She hastened

Samreen Chowdhury

Hastened

/ ˈheɪs(ə)n / **verb**
be quick to do something.

she hastened

Acknowledgements

In the name of Allah, whose mercy made this book possible. Peace and blessings upon His Nabi, prophet Muhammad ﷺ, whose account of hardships taught me to stay strong. I am sincerely grateful to all my prophets, whose way of life guided me to the path of faith and Amal (hope). To Abeer, who inspired me to become an open book, and to acquire knowledge. To my mother, whose tears and prayers saved me from drowning in the affairs of this Dunya. To my father, whose love fills the pages of this book. To Maryam, who carried me in my darkest nights, who heard me weep. To my soul friends whose intellect uplifts me. To Mohima, whose laughs glorified our broken pieces. I dedicate this book to all of you and those who are seeking the path of resonation of hope and despair. All praise is due to Allah, the Lord of the worlds.

she hastened

Contents

she hastened

she hastened

she hastened

she hastened

CHAPTER ONE

THE LOST SERIES

she hastened

Breakdown, 3.29 AM

My dreams sail through the storms of every day
My thoughts stay fixed in my head as I have nothing to say
I eat, sleep, educate and before you know it's a brand new day

Time hurries and while I chase the minutes, the hours, the seconds
I'm losing more and more
I'm out of breath.

I can't breathe and I'm drowning in this sort of horrific tribulation
there's nothing that I exactly need
Because there is a lost soul

I'm growing in pain and hurt
Living in distress and hurt
Sleeping in pain and hurt and if only—

If only you knew how many days I have released my tears
the hurt I feel from within
the darkness that invaded the only light I have left within me-

she hastened

Tears are words the heart can't express

Whitney Fancher

she hastened

A Rose with thorns

Strong but then weak

Happy but then disheartened

Sometimes feeling hopeful

But always dreading the bad

Scared and uncertain, *where will it end?*

Stress-free but distressed

Smiling but anxiety!

Loving but being hated against.

Loved but forgotten?

she hastened

my heart

she hastened

Sixteen

She's sixteen and can speak of self-destruction

In such intricate detail

She's learned how to hold all her

Feelings inside

Until she makes it late at night

She knows how to cover her mouth

So that no one may hear her

She's perfected her masking smile

She's been taught

So harshly

To build her walls up so high

To tuck away those cries

she hastened

You weren't for my growth, nor was I for yours
We were sure happy but
deep inside we remained wearily unhappy
So Allah had removed you from me
So that we could finally be at peace
To grow our internal spirits
Depart from this uneasy journey

MyHeart

A dimensional Realm

What's the guidance?
There's light
There are paths
We have to break it down like its finance
Look up, at the stars
Millions, posing a manner of bliss

Purely appetising
This you can't resist
I glare at a flower in a vars
Give a glimpse- it is just like the stars
Why is it so beautiful?

A simple flower yet so colourful
Can this be the guidance?
My vision is so clear
The mournful moon moans to the clouds and tilts
The moon is not happy
it's breaking the hearts into bits.

My secrets are deeply hidden, being aware it's all forbidden
Background violence and sirens. My eyes
witnessed this before my body dies
My blood is cold

she hastened

The reality

It isn't how it use to be
reflection and confessions
it doesn't work out anymore
because it's been used and worn

reflection on so many memories but
that one particular one that stops
your heart from beating
Beating the normal kind of way, because it
takes you back to that same moment
makes you happy again
makes you smile again

like the same way you did then
that one beautiful moment, in slow motion you
feel the beauty of lightness
but then you know it wasn't the reality

you remember those aren't the people
and the world no longer benefits you
your life isn't the same
And thoughts transcend

where you think what's the truth of it
something that's veiling the mark behind us
it's nothing
But maybe there is something

just the wind that watches us and the wind
that we watch, it's
the case of loving again, and maybe one day
the memories or maybe that one memory will

she hastened

become alive again

she hastened

Memories invaded

The photographs from the past years to recent
years tells a story, a love story
it begins with happiness and ends with a cry

regretting the things you've done causes pain to your instincts
and all the good things too
creating a carriage of mistakes
one of them was creating a bond between you and I or us

That was the biggest mistake, by letting go
You are creating a mind invaded by frustration, why?
these memories expressed in the photographs aren't just memories

they're special and every moment was cherished shown in the smiles
the foolish part of all of this is watching your world fall apart
The love journey has expired

she hastened

The pain from within

There is a pain within this heart
My pain within my sadness through my
eyes
My eyes are like a burden that you can
see right through me
That one single heart left behind
intoxicated and enclosed in fear
fear of darkness from within
No chance on the senses getting healed
shattered like a million pieces of glass
There's light, there is hope
and the happiness that I once wanted to feel
Now I only ever just feel this sadness
It is what I experience
from within
A pain within these doors I can hear it say
there is no way out
No way to wash away the pain
The pain I feel

she hastened

I can't go on

Forgiveness
to forever fall
there is only fear
a moment, an instant

Dearly departed

she hastened

Distance and difficulties

My eyes are fixed so beautifully on you
I'm looking right at you
but you're fading away and sometimes it feels like you're not here
I can sense your body and now I can visualise it
but your mind is somewhere else
It feels like you're so far gone
This thing inside me questions me
the thing that stops me from
breathing
because you're no longer here you
went away with an unknown
farewell
this distance between our souls
and this distance is painful
Things are not close but mirrored
Disconnection like a war strike
so unexpected

she hastened

CHAPTER TWO

THE THOUGHTS SERIES

she hastened

Dear Abu

A tribute to my dear sister, R

I can't shed any more tears
I've been crying, day in and day out
For you to come back
My world has become pitch black

I wish you could hold me again
In your arms
Hold me close to your heart
And call me your baby again

It is in your arms I cradled
Became the petals of the rose
You planted
Why did you go?

Now, who do I call Abu?

So soon, without leaving us with any words
I feel so lost without you
No one sees
How much I shed tears for you
As I lay in my bed in the darkness

I dread the next morning
Knowing that you will not be here
I will not hear your voice
Nor your precious laughs

she hastened

I can't tell you abu how many tears I have shed
Since the day I was told
That my precious father had died
I can't comprehend it still today
I still remember your eyes on that very day
It seems so impossible, my beloved
My first love, my first male role model
It seems so impossible

Although I know it's true
As everything, I see around
Reminds me of you

Your shoes, your coat
What you touched
you left everything behind
You told me not to ever cry
And I do not in front of people

Whilst we begged Allah for a miracle to come by
And pleaded to Him with every little hope we had in us
As they told us that there are now minutes remaining
The moment you left
We accepted the decree of Allah

The moment that changed my little world
My heart was gorging out my mouth
Tears streaming but no noise
Everything was in darkness
It was a sharp pain in the heart

you are not gone
in heaven, you await for us to reunite

she hastened

Heaven is so lucky to have you
I miss you so much
But at night I can't stop myself

You held my little hands when I was small
Had mercy on me when you first set your eyes on me
How I fell so in love with you
How I wish I could do everything you did for me
Before you had gone

I could only trace you back when my head is down
On the floor
In sujood
For moral support
I can't stop myself but cry
How could I not say goodbye?

Who else now do I call out to?

Abu, you wished to bid me farewell
On the night you were supposed to
give your precious daughter away
Abu my heart aches so much
Sometimes it hurts so much

I can't seem to carry on
I still hear your laughter
And envision your bright, smiling face
I still miss the sound of your gentle voice

The wisdom in your advice
The stories of your life
And just being in your presence

she hastened

Abu, they are counting the weeks, months

And years
but death only changes everything and time changes nothing
If only they knew
I miss you as much today
As I did the day you lost your heartbeats

On that hospital bed
I wish I was able to hold onto you for longer
But your soul became weaker
And it is Allah who chose this date for you

That Jannah will be promised for you
How your character was so perfect, merciful
Soft and kind
How they loved you ever so much
How it was on this day
The doors of Jahannam were closed for you

So Allah had mercy over you
Took you away to depart
From this Dunya
Where destruction lies
Where it's no longer even a Dunya today
Your warm heart
Your compassionate soul

Your love encompasses my body
Causes me to live on
Baba, this is the legacy you left behind!
Your love emanates my world
I just want to pour my heart out sometimes

she hastened

Release the screams and the constrictions in my throat
Which have built up
since the day you were pronounced dead on your deathbed
Not a day goes by that I don't think of you
You'll always be loved
The strongest thread in my duas
I just miss you

I miss every occasion I had with you
How every Eid you'd wrap your arms around me
Loved me, how can they not see
That I can not utter or speak
Upon the level of love you gave me

There is no other who is;
As forgiving as you
As pleasing as you
As eloquent speaking as you
How serene where those twinkling eyes which
reflected your peaceful attributes!

I wish I could hold onto you for the longest
But deep beneath the grounds, there you lay
It feels so cruel
But you rest as Allah has taken your soul away
Far away
In a land full of light
In a land full of delight

I have picked flowers for you
Placed them on your stone
Perhaps they'll keep you warm

she hastened

They are coloured, and I have beautified
This stone for you

So that the angels may protect and guard you
Abu. I'll make you so proud
And I can't wait to join you in the rivers of paradise
To tell you how far I've come

To forget all the misery I was in
As we rejoice Jannah together
As you hold me in your arms again
I can't wait to tell you how much I've missed you
How hard it's been
Without you

But I wear the smile you gave me and
I can't wait to find sanity
And the completeness in my soul again
When I lost you
At that moment, I am the one who didn't exist
But you do not belong to me
Or amu, or the rest of your daughters

You belong to Allah alone
إِنَّا لِلَّهِ وَإِنَّا إِلَيْهِ رَاجِعُونَ
And it is these words which regained the
life in me
Made me realise
That time is just passing by

And I cannot wait to go myself
I am so ready
Ready to join you, to be with you

she hastened

Run to you when I see you in the
distance

'Abu! Abu! Abu!'
And cry in unshakable happiness
In bliss
Find solace again
'Abu we made it'
And we will be one again
Reunite again
We will forget what pain and distress this day
Had caused
You wait for us in barzakh
We are coming

Ya Rab allow my fathers grave to widen
so that the perfume of paradise may reach every inch of the pit,
including the soil which he resides in today.
Ya rabbi make his ultimate journey easy for him,
he was my guardian, my saviour, my light
have mercy on him the way he had mercy on me.
Place him on top of the heavens and beyond, let him rejoice in
tranquillity and ease.

Dear readers, as you have come to the end of this devastating write, I
want your tongue to utter 'Ameen' with sincerity out loud so that your
'Ameen' is followed by the 'Ameen' of the angels listening to the symphony
of the cries inside of you right now.

First, gather your thoughts and feel the constriction in your throat, feel the
heavy heart gorging out of its place and remember the loneliness of this
mu'mins (believer) pit. We lose many members of the ummah every day,
but here is one who Allah gave all services to and the best of deaths, here is

she hastened

one who we must strive to follow the footsteps in as to be blessed with a death like this, he is only the friend of Allah, know that these are only a minority! So go cry for your soul to rest this way, for Allah to gift these services to you too, for Allah to love you as much as he had loved this believers heart so dearly and to have returned his slave to Him in such a beautiful way...

You may utter the word when your heart is ready to pour out its sincerity...

AMEEN.

Your daughter, Rehana.

she hastened

*'And we will surely test you with something of **fear** and **hunger** and a loss of **wealth** and **lives** and **fruits**. But give good tidings to the patient.'*

Quran 2:155

she hastened

but I lost myself when I lost you

she hastened

Dear anxiety

I do not pity you nor do I hate you
I understand the reason behind why you were created
and I understand why fear is your close friend
but don't you realise the hurt you are making me go through?

Don't you care about the toxic emotions my entire body is fuelling up to?
I'm physically restrained
I have become a feral child, I have a fear of being alone
a fear of standing, walking

Old age

The wrinkles on my skin make me feel young in the sun
even though I'm old
The sun is so beautiful so it attracts me in every way
While In our teens, everything seems to be great
but when we reach the age of 20 things seem to occur as fate

We begin to love as it's our human nature
but once it's broken we hold grudges
So at 30, We distrust and 40 we hide and make experiences to learn

Eventually, at 50 we go downhill until we reach 60 and lose our will
They say at 70 it's time and slowly at 80, we've lost our mind

Life makes us have a morality that's filled with inspiration and thoughts
old experiences and love
So we let go and let the cycles of birth to old age happen, over time

she hastened

Precious pearls

She stared directly into herself in the mirror
She smiled ever so much
Tomorrow was her first visit from the nurse

And she placed her hands on her back
tilted herself to the left as she stood a little back
To make a firm observation
She outlined her growing stomach with her index finger

Safe and sound was the baby
Her baby
In the womb, he grew
safe from the world and safe from catastrophes

she hastened

'If I lost you and Mohima,
it would be like losing both my eyes,
I would no longer be able to see the world'.

My beloved father.

she hastened

Just another night

And they just flow
like the raindrops that fall on the roof of the umbrellas
And it hurts to think days like this won't come back
days like this will become the 'past'

How we just go through paths that lead us to different idyllic universes
How closeness can lead to loneliness
Happiness lasts only for a little while

How God knows I'm trying but no one can see the struggle within
the emotion within, how it feels so invisible
How pride gets all swallowed up

How we don't let the hurt show,
Because people just don't want to know
How looking into people's eyes you just can't believe

she hastened

Stay focused

Stop penetrating my mind excessively
I don't want to be a part of you
because I know I won't be able to be me
I don't want to shut my eyes and be isolated
I want to be able to live and be free
I want to be able to believe and see
See the things that I didn't see before
with you, it's all a lie, promises
and the wounds that you've created for me
You've entirely belittled and shamed me
I can't trust you or be focused on only you
you snatched things away from me
I'm drifting away, far
away from you
I'm holding onto
Nothing

she hastened

Mental prison

Imprisonment of the mind is what I face
tormenting thoughts I cannot escape
the battle of my life is taking place
There is not enough space to ease my heart's pace

I have conversations with suicide
I keep rejecting the honour to have an insight
I had a dream that my ways were getting better
suddenly perfecting
It's a lie

Thoughts of you visit me during my weakest moments
promising me you can make me free from torment
I dangerously flirt with your cutting smile
it's just a hallucination, a doom of a delusional experience

Just an image of your dark style
I'm searching my mind, trying to find something positive to focus on
I catch a thought but it doesn't last for long
Loneliness has taken its toll
emptiness has scarred my soul
Thoughts of you never cease
and each day of my life feels severely incomplete

she hastened

Helpless

Fighting for me has now become an addiction

fighting and fighting for the rights of others around me
good morning
I've had a wrecked and sleepless night but I look forward to every single
day
I glare into the window and watch the freedom of birds
I pray that I become a bird one day
My soul is controlled but my emotions are awakened
taking a deep breath. In and out, slowly
I could hear the rustling sounds of winds through my throat
curling my fists, vibrating my heart in anger
my vision changes into blurs
a stream of tears

she hastened

I wish I had freedom

Up and down. Up and down

They move me up and down
yes. I'm a puppet, attached to two elastic strings
and there's nothing that I'm allowed
they pull me
every day and some days all-day
My body is weakened
It happened yesterday too and the night before
It happens every day
there's nothing that I could say
I want to cry
I want to scream
but they took my voice away
I wish I could be wild and free
dance through the howling trees every single day
But no. I'm a puppet that's controlled
This is not a story, nor is it a fairytale

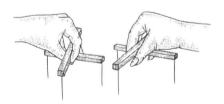

she hastened

Change

All of us experience change in our lives
Change is the one constant in our lives
There are changes that we look forward to and change that we fear
one thing is for sure-
Things will not stay the same
no matter how much we would like them to
When a life change occurs, we have two choices in how to respond;
We can despair that a change has come
and assume that things will be worse;
or we can look with excitement
at the new possibilities that the change presents

she hastened

Sudden sadness

I cry a river, no one can listen
Silent tears
I cry a river no one can feel
Inside it's trying to heal
Just colours of dark, grey and black fill
the world in which I live
My smile is nothing of what it seems
Soul captured, freedom enclosed
Fortitude in my tears
But cries due to my fears
Empty, loneliness and solitude
My shadow fights
There's a decline in eyesight
Shadows of darkness invade
I cry a river and no one hears

she hastened

No peace

My trembling fingers allocates the screen
Abusive words begin to pierce profoundly
I give in all and take a deep breath
My stomach rumbles

It's the bears screeching for peace, there's no peace
As the tears roll down my cheeks
I have no answer to my mind full of unspoken questions
I break through the silence with earphones

I begin to curl up like a relentless kitten
almost being pulled to be eaten by its prey
I'm so stuck to the imprisonment
my body faces on a daily basis
how my mind and thoughts are latched onto nothing

but an empty box
Closed and unilluminated
Neglectful horror crosses my emotions
and I am now conjoined into a double life
Freedom is what I crave

yearn every single day
I grew whilst being intellectually broken
damaged profusely

through a chain of events
but that has been taken away. Snatched
A feral human
Abandoned and caressed by darkness
my vision deepens

she hastened

there is no light commencing in me
My voice is not to be heard
and my hands are tied up onto a horizon seat

she hastened

Content

You may not be able to bury your hardest times
forgetting that they happened
that it did break your heart
Or change then down the line
because those times were hard

they'll endure the moments
when you realise you are strong enough
when you know you made it
until the very end of the chapter titled *'misery'*
you realise that you are strong enough to stand on top of them

I wore my strongest posture and smiled so hard
and I've achieved something
I've achieved a range of mountains which I learned to climb
and I'll keep climbing to the top until finally
I'll say, *'I made it'*

Pain

My dreams sail through the storms of everyday
My thoughts stay fixed in my head
as I have nothing to say
I eat, sleep, educate and before you know it's a brand new day
Time hurries and while I chase the minutes

the hours, the seconds
I'm losing more and more
I'm out of breath
I can't breathe and I'm drowning in this sort of horrific pain
there's nothing that I exactly need

Because I'm born into pain
I'm growing in pain and hurt
Living in pain and hurt
Sleeping in pain and hurt and if only

If only you knew how
How hurt the heart was
What distress it was in
the hurt I feel from within
the darkness that invades the only light I have
left within me

she hastened

صبر

Patience

she hastened

Trailing thoughts

Some nights I do wonder
And other nights I drift off to perishing dreams
I shouldn't care less or maybe I should
Sweet roses have petals but they do have thorns too

Oceans are blue
but deep down they contain things that undermine our imaginations
reality becomes untrue
Untold stories remain a secret
But do secrets ever last?
And my shrines will uncover and maybe he will say at last

Devotions above values
And things just get too over-boarded
Like valleys so vast
Pretty nest, nurturing baby bluebirds but will they get any worms since
they are working, on task?

The sky is so bright with sunshine's delight
and at night do the stars collide
I will not tell you what lays behind the mist, the big moon
As she mantles with the dark gloomy sky

she hastened

On a summers day, in July, I had been told upon expressing my frustration,

'And when it pours down in rain, know that it is the mercy of Allah, the plants too need food and drink. We cannot live in selfishness'.

My beloved aunty, an imitation of my dear mother.

she hastened

A pretty soul

An incomplete soul
A gap in the heart
A stab in emotion

Every inch of my body is tightened
Twisted, relentlessly
Sabotaging my inner peace dug deep in

As I shut my eyes
I fear the darkness and the woe of intense grief
misery and sorrow

Don't pity me
I'll do it on my own
Don't come near me
I got this on my own

They let this upheaval unravel
but this adversity will be annihilated
And I will not be festered
Because of this Higher power
I am fastened
And you can break me but someone else will piece me

I am indeed perturbed
but through this heart-wrenching trauma
I will breakthrough
And you cannot conceal
my wounds because of how skin-deep cut they are
But for sure they will speak

They will speak and they will be scars of wisdom

she hastened

strength and
A clear sign of how time has elapsed

Drifted dreams

Freedom is solely an illusion
I dream of freedom
To spread my wings one day
I pray I pray, I pray

To one day
Subvert to this binding element
To this dictatorship
To spread my wings, To the air, I will cling

To the wind, that will help illuminate my soul
I will wait and wait. Because right now there's no exception
but to accept this displeasing fate

she hastened

Invasion

Memories blur the mind
But the thoughts caress the frail heart
Tears forget the bliss
And tomorrow's another night

Her heart beats so hard
As she hurts in discomfort
For the thoughts that do not make sense
For the thoughts that do not chain up

And the tears fall
As they become so close incall
And they fall and fall

she hastened

Mental health

Issues. You helped at first gave me the lot
A spade to bury you know what
Adding a little numbness to my pain
Which drink will you pour me today?
What drug takes me furthest away
From horrors ripping lumps out of my brain

I'm sorry are you losing track?
My moods swing to the moon and back
Crash Landing on the closest loved one's head
I do talk when I isolate
There's no one coming it's too late
I'll play some death by a duvet in my bed
Come out now coward let's all see
What takes complete control of me
Destroying hope whilst pissing on my dreams

Emotions shielded by your code
Brought on my latest episode
The one where nothing's ever as it seems
Of course a giant I should have known
I'd no idea how much you'd grown
You hold the ace with every other card
You're out now though and have been seen

My cut shall be slowly clean
Until you catch me once again- off guard

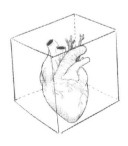

she hastened

The older we get, you realise your heart has outgrown the instances of life, you've watched so much. Endured so much. There is nothing more to say. Your delinquency is remembered as stupidity but that is part of your story. The more you grow your intellect, the less you care, and the less you utilise your speech.

she hastened

CHAPTER THREE

THE SEXUAL HARASSMENT SERIES

she hastened

Hastened against her will

My hands were tied

My mouth was sealed by his skin

Sweating hands

Agitating to get his task done

He said if I scream he'll strangle me

He said if I make a sound he'll hasten me

To submit to him

To his whims

To his desires

What a mournful regret I was in

To have made it to my chamber

To rest for the night

In peace- sleep has broken its treaty

With peace

she hastened

There is no peace in sleep

In blankets

In duvets

In pillows

When every night it'll remind you of the darkness

That had occurred

Even when it's no longer occurring

He told me to stay quiet until he's done with me

So with a reluctant speed, he kept going

Until I whimpered in pain

And in stylistic agony

Sadistic was his flesh in me

I had forgotten what realm I was in

As every good and innocence in me

had become worn down

My skin was drowning in disgust

she hastened

I had no tears

As it's already coming to an end

There was not much time remaining

He grunted as he removed his pressed down hands off my mouth

And he touched my brown strands of hair from the front

Messy from the silent nodding no's

Gently grazing them with his fingers

Pinched them

And put them behind my ear very gently

To carve a path for himself to draw himself

Closer to the same ear

And whisper

If you tell anyone you'll not remain alive

And off he went

Banished himself

she hastened

From my private chamber

she hastened

Why did you break into me?

They'll make you feel special at first
But then they'll plot a game to play with you
You feel safe
Because they are yours, not your enemy

But they'll touch you in ways
Which you are not sure it's wrong
You try to move
But it's been so long

So long trying to figure out if it's wrong
They make normal situations feel uncomfortable
All the teasing
The sex talking

The gifts and whispers
It's so easy to spot when others go through it
But you fall silent when it is you who becomes the victim

I didn't want him to be in the wrong
Or get into trouble
I didn't want anyone thinking different about him
I just wanted things to be normal again

To forget everything
But I let it go on for so long
Maybe it was my fault?
I spent months thinking I'd keep this a secret
Forever
But I couldn't hide from him
I held on for so long
But it was breaking me

she hastened

I couldn't think straight day and night
One morning I said
"Mom I need to tell you something"
And the tears streamed down as I lost the words and voice to speak

She comforted me before I had the chance to again speak
I called out the truth
He let me confide in him

I wasn't fond of it?
I wasn't
I felt disturbed
In my mind, in my body, in my health

He wrapped me around his arms
Held me tight
Grazed his body feature against mine
I wanted to break out from his arms

I thought it was fine?
But it didn't feel normal
Nor comfortable
What was he doing?

I felt so confused

she hastened

Note: This is a fictional poem, influenced by the authors reading of a non-fiction book, 'the imam's daughter' by Hannah Shah.

My father played a game called 'monsters'

I can smell the disgust
My fingers are forced around his flesh
My dad played 'monsters'
when I was 7, I was good. He said I'll go to heaven.
It was a game
Everyone thought the same
In reality, I hear the heavy breathing
The demons sound like a strangled Raven
My fingers wrapped around the rustling shawl
I'm forced right down
Now stuck on this wooden bed
So hard that from years it has lost its spark
This point deep inside me
Reddening my face
Thickening my blood
It flowed out my eyes
With reluctant speed
I was pleasured in horror and distress
I scream in fear
I feel so much pain
Immortal thoughts filling my brain
He told me to call him dad
What such thing did I pose which was bad?
Monsters-I don't like monsters
It haunts me
I'm shivering in an empty room
This place is so cold and ungodly
I tremble through this wrenching grave
This is my monster father

she hastened

Sexual harassment

Did you ever wonder why I'm feeling this way when he's talking to me?
Why is it that my nerves tremble when he comes near me?

Why's it that I'm the one getting crept upon
whilst everyone is being happy and free?
Why am I becoming so overburdened?

What the eyes hold
Is very bold
I watched you

You crept over me
In silence and broke into me
Where did you find this key?

Can't think straight
Why did you choose me?
As your victim, as your predator

Once this night ends
Tomorrow will begin a new day
Silence will occur
As if nothing had occurred

I'm about to sit in the bathtub
Wash out this night from my skin
My body, my hair

she hastened

They let me die; Rape scene

One more scream
One last shout
One last *"help"*
Nothing, no one came for me
I stopped breathing normally
I cried in horror
I moved around unusual bones in despair
There was no one out there that cared

she hastened

2.30 AM

My body is the stranded landscape
Over which you wish to roam, tread, touch and feel
Silent I am, with small heartbeats
abyss amid darkness

hesitant as I hear you breathe
My body for you is so free
To explore
To see

To discover
Your new territory
To claim it as yours
to embrace and glorify the skin as your treasuring seas

Just a little more while until I am set free
2.40, I may let you enjoy but I am torn up and casketed
sealed and so bruised
It's just another time, another day
of your invasion, I can't heal

she hastened

Broken season

Tonight she glared upon the sky
Watched the twinkled stars, make tweaks
To the beautiful sky

Lit up
So bright and dazzled her eyes

As it watches over her
The wind emanates her flowing garb
She walks into the distance
wherein there is darkness

But a lit up moon,
So still and lonely.

she hastened

A beloved heart
So kind and so endearing
Her words- so profound
Her tears in mine, and mine in hers
'I'll be here for you no matter what'
Maryam

she hastened

CHAPTER FOUR

THE HEREAFTER SERIES

she hastened

Departure

She awaits her eternal abode
She waits to see the doors of paradise
She awaits her arrival and her shade under the bright sun

Her mayhem will be over
As she descends into the pit
Her adornment of light grows inside

Flitting will be this light
Streaming from an unknown universe
so do not cry when she is gone

do not want her back
She is happy in her place
In her grave

She has been set free
From this disgruntled world
Unperturbed was her soul

So troubled and passively careless
Exhausted was she
It's time now to break
free

she hastened

A traveller in the land

This world is like a sinking ship
The more you indulge
the deeper you delve into the depths of the oceans
and lose sense as the waves suffocate you

she hastened

Hidayah (Guidance)

Direction-I can't seem to find pleasure in the laughter of others
I can't find heed through the speech of Mankind
There seems to be something obstructing my contentment-
it's the Dunya
Surely it is
It is only through You
where I feel the materialism dusts off and becomes clear air
melting into the horizon and deep within the oceans
becoming my strength although
it's much lofty than me
It's the value of each individual which is considerate
maybe solely, and it is not entirely the size or the outward appearance
It is simply the weight of Iman
And even if there is none
but there is a beating heart who holds an atom's weight of Iman
He will take in this man carrying the weight of the atom

she hastened

Al-Zuhd (one who is deeply ready for the hereafter)

A land full of deen
No pain no misery
A land full of light, abundance and eternal bliss
A land where there is no destruction
A new realm with unimaginable colours
Filled with humble companions who speak of deen
I wish I could explain
I wish I had the words
But things feel so strange
I feel like a stranger in the land
Things are so difficult in this Dunya
Ya Rab, you know what lies in my heart
Please grant me my needs
please take the Dunya away from me
no more stops ya rab, take me back

she hastened

In this world

I am just a traveller passing by
I'm a stranger to every other member
I carry an empty luggage
My belongings are in my heart
I take heed through ilm (knowledge) alone
It is my only adornment too
My path is dictated by helpful companions
who assist me in this path
I'm travelling day and night
heading towards my final destination (The Akhirah)
I stop from time to time
but it is so I can collect my supplies
to continue with my journey

she hastened

Ya Rab

I know you hear me
My Lord, bring me back to you, close to you
beneath my heart where my chest is beating solely for you
far away from the darkness and emptiness, this Dunya brings
I'm ready to surrender to you, to provide my love to you
I was busy watching others walk ahead
in things that were not enough for the Akhirah
now I'm trying to repair the damages created and trying
to rejuvenate from the wounds
carved from the past that I have lived
I am scarred, broken and shattered
I can't cultivate it into words
but I can only release tears
because my heart has become so soft and fragile
so frail and only you understand ya rab, so I cry to you Alone
and each teardrop
only you comprehend so please suffice for me
and bring this calamity to an end

she hastened

Loneliness

You may feel alone, neglected and lonely in this journey
this beautiful journey to your lord
a journey where you are perfecting your Deen and renewing your
Iman and begging your Rab for His mercy

You feel as if you are on another page
maybe on the wrong page
Here is the truth, you've been blessed because Allah has chosen
you to be a traveller
a traveller in this Dunya and not amongst those who found
enjoyment in this fleeting world

Your heart is at its right place
To feel alone in a hostile world is a display of where your heart
rests and that's the eternal life- the Akirah

she hastened

Recently, I've been finding the corners of this world so cold and every time I search for the solace it seems to turn into nothing but misery. Nothing lasts. Things feel so cold and empty to the point where when I touch it...I crave the warmth of paradise more. Somewhere deep within there lies conceited happiness, though it is preserved for the afterlife. I was told there are three things you must uphold by my father: your religion, your character and your legacy.

she hastened

'be in this world as if you were a stranger or a traveller'
Prophet Muhammad ﷺ
Bukhari 6416

she hastened

CHAPTER FIVE

THE SLAVE TRADE SERIES

Redemption, a legacy of the slave trade

Silent tears

Rotting my heart and decaying my skin
Soaked in hardship and neglecting emotion
I cannot take on this notion of a battlefield any further

My mother- the last glimpse of her was when my eyes fixated on
her body language, scrunching up as I was being sold
To who I regard as my master today

Her hair a broomstick-
But she was ever so beautiful

To me, it looked like she was screaming as her mouth gaped wide
like she was in pain like she was suffering
Like she was getting abused internally

I transformed into a dumb character
Unable to speak or listen to the scream or the sound of the dismal
death which echoes still in my dreams

she named me Aaryan
It derived from being glorious
But do not glorify me as I tell you my story

I am not a commodity
I have been neglected from liberty
from being free

Physically I am burdened under a roof

she hastened

happiness displays but from within there's darkness and from
dusk till dawn
her tears sway like trees down her sweet rosy cheeks

but her devotion forces her to wipe it away
but still relentlessly, carelessly they fall constantly
And as she sits in prayer, the light focuses on her wherein there's
only darkness around her

completely broken she weeps in silence for better days, for hope-
for another world
But overshadowed by the domestic trauma where she was
drowned in abuse and misery

If she knew from the day she was conceived and born into this
A world full of lies
And today she has become the history

Distributed onto the papers
The greatest woman that ever lived,
'SHE diminished the slave trade of this great oppression'

She was the last one standing
For her master that proclaimed she wasn't the best, via his
commands
She has a trail, and a story to tell

And today her tortured but the valuable body is carried onto the
land of America
To be buried and hushed into some kind of
Coffin, without her justice being justified
Her body being concealed in soil

she hastened

1619 captured; the middle passage

I'm trembling, I seem to be always terror-stricken
I'm always looking over my shoulder and both left and right
So much abhorrence from my master, he hates me
Tormenting me at his whim

I sometimes ponder on who he will attack next
I hope I am not on his mind. I'm so sick of it being me
I try to escape and I try to hide
But when I do I am whipped beaten

that is the reassurance of my masters' domination
He always seems to know how to find me
I dream of freedom, liberty and tranquillity
Freedom is Elusive

Or perhaps an illusion

At every turn it bypasses
What's Hope?
My master, to him I am submissive
he owns me and therefore imprisons me
He has stolen my dignity and emotion

He would have me destitute
Alone, shackled to a nightmare
He robs me of life and flesh
He leaves me with no respect
My master is sin, greed and lust

I hate him as much as I disregard myself
payment is being made

she hastened

Another master beckons me
So I am free to follow, free to obey
free to be his slave, shackled to his walls of shame
True freedom: a pure illusion

There is no escape and I am stuck
I will always have a master
The tears come once again...He has now transacted the deceitful
payment for me and I hear him

Simply asks gently that I follow Him home
I am bought and purchased like a mere pet or object
Yet he still asks! He says he will lead me
direct me, guide me, HELP me, find me
More tears lapse

I saith a prayer; protect me, restore me. Save me, dear lord
He told me he will Love me! As a child - - and treat me like I am
his, I won't be condoned
An impossible affection for an unlikely recipient
Freedom is just an illusion. But Love? Perhaps that is existent

I hope it is real. I want it to be real
I need it to be real. I am aware that I am willing to change it
And so I subserviently agree to a transfer of ownership
 even though I haven't been given a choice

But it's just my illusion
When he calls. I will follow
When he asks, I will obey
He will be my master and my father
And I will be both his daughter and slave
Freedom: an illusion

she hastened

CHAPTER SIX

THE DEATH SERIES

she hastened

Gravestone #1

I call out to you. I say I love you. There is an echo in my heart. And I need you. But you wait for me in Barzaq (the barrier/waiting area). Smile, Jannah holds flowers for you, I'll be right behind you.

she hastened

Gravestone #2

There's a gravestone.

Engraved is your name. I come close to you, I place my hand where your heart lays beneath the soil. I want to lift you off this dirty ground. But death has no mercy. Death is a mockery. I feel connected to you. Until I call out your name, and there is no response. I turn my back and let my tears stream but don't let you watch.

she hastened

Gravestone #3

Today I decided to sit beside you for a longer period. It's been long since I spoke to you. It's been long since I heard your voice or heard you laugh. How are you? **There is no response.** *You taught me everything but I think you forgot to teach me how to live without you.*

she hastened

NoorInMyHeart,

When our hearts were being repaired upon when we made supplications, the angels heard our cries and delivered the message to Allah Rabbul izza', Allah then knew what pain the hearts were in, so He reunited the two. He had Mercy over me and you.

وَقَالَ رَبُّكُمُ ادْعُونِي أَسْتَجِبْ لَكُمْ ۚ إِنَّ الَّذِينَ

Call upon me; I will respond to you

(Qur'an 40:60)

she hastened

In the pit.

Deep within, there you lay. Beneath the ground, penetrated in the soil, the mud mixed with worms and insects. Just darkness. Every day I make footsteps to you, I place a rose on top of your stone. I wish you could see them. I wish you could smell them. They were picked out especially for you. Come back I need you.

she hastened

CHAPTER SEVEN

THE HOPE SERIES

she hastened

Oppression

She's hostage, yet her soul is so bright
So enlightened, so entranced
By the hope, her Lord brings to her thoughts and echoes

The waves pass by
yet she remains so faithful in her beliefs, In the destructions
In this great catastrophe

And soon it will be over
her heart yawns
She keeps going

she hastened

Progress

I've come this far
No one has told me
I am now set free
No one has told me
I've held onto my wings for so long
Now the wind is my bound, to it, I sing a lullaby
To it, I am bound
To it, I'll never let go
Don't cause me to fret
Let me go slow
You don't know
How much her heart was overburdened
But do not despair, she is both wise and young
And for what's to come, they'll be stunned

she hastened

A different perspective

There has been an undeniable truth
Since before we even existed;
Nothing ever stays the same
Change cannot be resisted

Now I shudder
In crowded places as noises aided to be too huge
Escaped and fled to the silence of sweet solitude
Feel the rhythm, feel the beat

Of the soul retracting and to its retreat
Hinder souls and break free

Healing wounds

My dear darling

Please be gentle

Be always gentle

With me

My soul hides so many wounds

That never bleed

Did you hear me?

Be gentle, my love

My heart is weakened

It's conditioned

It's searching

It's in disguise

concealing the hardships

So be so gentle my love

she hastened

After every hardship comes ease

Some nights I use to drift off into thoughts
and others I wept until my eyes shut.
All the toil
the hardship and pain

'Bare patience my dear slave
I will give in good timing' is what I lived by
I wonder how them times have left

I drift into laughter and I do wonder
How we have come out of this great tempest
How Allah said He will give and He gave

O how Allah works in such mysterious ways!

How my tears rolled down in sadness and pain
For things to just change; and 'ya rajai' (oh my hope) I said with
conviction
and so much pain, with the words as constriction in my throat

If only I knew those nights,
He was so close to me, listening to me
My rab, my merciful Allah, my beloved

He is the best of all listeners
He heard my voice
He granted my intimate prayers

she hastened

All praise is due to Allah, The Lord of the Worlds.

she hastened

Solace

There was a tall red rose
I saw it's shattered beauty hung
Upon an injured stem
And I heard them say
'what need to care when there is rose budding everywhere?'
I remained silent in their words

There was once a bird
Carried down to die
I heard them say
'what reason to be disheartened when hundreds fill the sky?'
I remained silent in their words

There was a little girl
Who's lover had let her down, banished was he
I heard them talk
'do not fret, there are plenty of gentlemen for you out there to choose from'
I smiled

she hastened

Don't be afraid

She's been told to not be afraid
Through the sweet words of her mother
Her gentle kindness

Her unforgettable sacrifices
Yet she watched her weep in the abyss
She raised her own hands for it to be all over

She whispered faintly, but the angels heard her and followed her 'Ameen'
with their sacred 'Ameen'
It had become an obligation upon them

To send this letter to the Lord of the worlds
For a request
To finally set them free

And if only they knew Allah had smiled
Freedom is what they were going to feel
and finally, see

she hastened

If only she knew

She holds onto the thin ropes
She cried for so long
The road seemed so long
there was a flag she could see

That marked her victory
It has now inflated. Into a blur
She's crying and she is so hurt

But she's doing well
she's about to make it
there remains only a little bit

She grasps onto the little hope she saved last night
She keeps fighting like it's her last fight
she's doing well, if only it was all in her sight

her happiness is about to be granted
If only she knew that there are only a few
A few that hurt so much as she did
she endured so much
but farewell to her sorrows she was about to bid and rid

If only she knew

she hastened

Somewhere deep down you may find my heart. It has sunk. I have nowhere to go, the road seems so long but I keep holding on. I wish someone could pick me up and let me spread through the flittering winds. Trying to navigate through to hear the birds sing. I can't keep going, I know that I am trying but it is so tiring.

she hastened

1.25 AM

Drowning in this hardship
Crying
But no one hears me

A knot in my throat
A knot needing to be released
A burden
A broken soul

My hope- Allah

she hastened

Regrets but hopes

The regret torments my mind
I wish I could undo and re-establish the way of life

I lost control of myself and my insecurities have deepened
When I speak, there is no longer any value
the tone is higher and I only realise I'm speaking loud when someone
else recognises it- anxiety

Now anxiety churns in my stomach and perpetuates immensely
this leads to nothing
but nervousness and a lack of empathy towards concepts and people
a lack of emotion

There's a lot of wishes and hopes
but I've tied so many knots and
surely after every hardship comes ease, Allah will provide

He is the sustainer
Allah will protect, He is the most merciful
Allah will love, He is the most benevolent

she hastened

Inner peace from within comes from iman and an unsullied character. A heart that is devoted and sincere, loyal to the creator, is ahead of the game in this Dunya, preparing for the Akirah. Their hearts beat for The Almighty, the Gafoor and Al Raheem, in the plight of an audience who are after worldly desires.

she hastened

Reignite your heart

Remove the fire in your eyes with the tears
let it be your hero
let it be your distinguisher

Smile from within not to paint a mask
Look around you, be grateful for things you have
and forget the things you don't have
Let that be your motivation, your dedication, your effort and hard work

Embrace what you have and don't envy your blessings
Look at your mother
that's your greatest blessing
the woman who structured your soul

Look at your father
the first man who fell in love with you
from the moment you came into this world

The upbringing from pure love
the greatest blessing that is
You are loved
you are beautiful and you are worth it

she hastened

4:29 AM

It's just another night where my pillow is soaked with woeful tears
It's dark, muted and sombre
relentlessly the tears lapse
one by one with a meaning attached to every tear,

quietly creating a strange rhythm sounding quite horrific to consider
Motionlessly I grab the duvets with fuelled moistness
and aggression for the melancholy emotion to come to an end
I wish I were as brave as the rain because they are not afraid to fall

I've lost the courage and strength to make it to a victory
But here I'll speak for the many figures who have lost voices just like me
you are not alone, and someday you'll heal
So wipe away those mortal tears and fuel yourself with God's love, grace
and intimacy
you are worth it

she hastened

Dear Allah

Ya Rajai' (my Hope) as I lay here in silence, I ask you to please recover my woes and bring back my living self to a better state. Aameen.

Dear Al Fattah; the great opener,

Heal me and halt my griefs. Please soak up my tears and take me back to my happiness, take me back to the light, take me back to a sincere state of mind.

she hastened

One day

And one day

One day, not in this Dunya

But in another, Allah will provide ease, and wash away all worries

So let those tears fall, they befit you

They were designed for you

And the victory is near

نصر من الله والفتح كريم

Help from Allah and a near victory

(Quran 61:13)

she hastened

Strength

Maybe I was tarnished
Maybe you kept my heart hostage
you left me with no voice, voiceless
I continued this magnitude of loss
grief and this ongoing, perpetuating journey
Maybe I was shattered
like silent glass shatteringly causing distress
But you are who made me
You moulded me
You took me back to my Lord

She's crying

Oh, Allah, my heart is breaking
I have no one else to call out to but You
Please help me, please pick me up
Please remove these heavy burdens and hardships
my heart aches so much
Ya rab feed me with your solace
let me live in light, not darkness

she hastened

CHAPTER EIGHT

THE LOVE LETTER SERIES

she hastened

Only with you

I rest my head on your beating chest and feel every heartbeat, and as I lean in more closely with proximity, there seems to be a skip in the beats. Surely we were meant to be. Because it is my heart too that skips a beat.

she hastened

Signals

Do you hear those signals?
Maybe those are your signs
The pain? Maybe it's the messengers

Keep close to them
Feel the rhythm and do not despair
Let your heartbreak, so that it may open

So keep it open and do not hide
Do not hide from the night
Do you see the moon?

You want the moon
So do not hide from the night

she hastened

Soulmate

Whilst the skies were being mantled
Before the stars had risen and placed into position
Fifty thousand years ago
My beloved

Before the moon was designed
Allah, the sublime, had created you for me
And so this story is glorious
This story is profound

And Allah only knows
when and where
it will begin and end

she hastened

tears are prayers too when you can't speak

she hastened

A Night like this

A secret prayer for my beloved
As the night sky transitions into pitch-black
As my head rests on these soft pillows
As the blanket covers my shivers
I utter a whisper

A small prayer
Upon my beloved
Under the same sky, we live
Under the same moon, we sleep

Night my beloved

Reason is powerless in the expression of love
Rumi

she hastened

Love letters

She's standing there setting the sunshine
She's shining, beauty is what she defined
He truly falls for that smile
with you only as a gift and surprise

I can see it clearly as a day
shining from your soul
hiding from the prey
it truly makes you whole

so wipe away your tears
set your beauty free
leave behind your fears
walk away

she hastened

in your arms, I forgot the world

she hastened

Goodbye, my love

Time is precious, as life slips away
for the hopelessness eats away
the pain burns
I am but a lost soul
your feelings faded by the years
for the pain eats away

But I don't want to live
without a dream
Goodbye, my love

she hastened

'Ana w-qalbi

Some nights you'll find me wondering
Hoping
With you, with the wind
Hoping

That God wills it and I can be near you
Oh my heart look what disdain
This love has put me in
Such unease

Above a clear sea whose waves carried me along
For so long
It had followed the scent of love
Through the soft winds
Gently

And near you dropped me
Lifelessly
It said farewell to me
And had left me here alone

After warning me
That this will hurt, and to you, I am bound
And to you, I'll find hurt
But deep love

Some type of unbreakable connection
Some type of knotted bond
It had warned me and said
"Don't ever forget your lover"

Oh, my heart

she hastened

Look what you did to us?
We are so lost, so indulged
I and my heart searched a lifelong

For you
My love
Now that you are here
hope needs to get stronger
So I could forget this pain

she hastened

And to Allah (alone) we seek for help, for alone only we understand, our struggles of each day and night. And so Allah alone will listen. And the waves will one day disappear.

she hastened

We met but countless Years ago, our Maker paired us with proximity and He chose you for me.

she hastened

Anti habibati antee

I have died for myself and I have only lived for you
I have
I have no words
It's felt in my heart, so close, so intimate
In my bones, in my blood
My love for you
Is higher than words
So I have decided to fall silent

she hastened

I will ask Allah for you twice, once in this Dunya, and once in Jannah
Fid Dunya wal akhirah.

she hastened

Two doves

Together we'll build our wings and we'll fly out one day
feel the essence of freedom
We'll release ourselves and put our hearts to peace
a little more patience and we'll set ourselves free
He will have mercy on us and promises from Him

Will never be broken
whether it's for this world or the next
Both of these Dunya together we'll succeed
Keep on going
the road is long but this sadness will only make you strong
this hatred will only make you stand up
don't take it for granted
there's no such thing as weakness

she hastened

A letter to him

To the love of my life

Somewhere out there you exist. In my heart I have you and on my mind are thoughts of you and our future. Our offsprings running around with your glimmering eyes and your soul that's complete enough for the ocean, a human being created with love. Whoever you are. Whatever walks in life. By the best of All writers. We will have a promised eternity together. Pure bliss. We will sure uplift each other and make it through rough times. I have my goals and you have yours- we will complete it together. For us, for the people around us, for our children. For Allah. For love. I want to build an empire with you. I want to travel the world, learn about the earth's history and explore nature. I want to be humble and understanding. I want to be beautiful with you, and for you. I want to grow with you. Today I pray for you, and Tomorrow will be the day I pray with you. Our heads together in sujood, in the pleasure of Allah and gratitude for the moment of relief.

Yours.

she hastened

To the segments of my soul

I have cried more than I laughed
Argued more than I spoke eloquently
but through it all, you were the one who understood my speech
even when I was voiceless
you were the one who voiced me
and untangled the knot with the love you held for me
And by the expression I held, you knew that there was a storm prevailing
but you asked me 'are you okay?' as you winged me
you let me cry on your shoulders and used your words to rejuvenate me

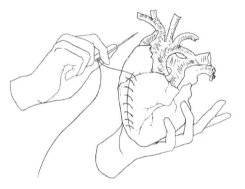

she hastened

Companionship

Feel the shudder in your shoulder
Deep deep
Feel it in your veins
Your bones
And blood

Hear the laughter and forget
Feel the signals
The connections
Deep sense

Feel the vibrations
The intuition
Feel the pull
Let them let you in
Hear the music of their soul

Let them call you
Let them signal you
Rill reap through the air
And dance through
Forget

Ensure you do not have a clue

she hastened

CHAPTER NINE

THE DA'WAH SERIES

she hastened

Youth

I am young and I have desires
I have tendencies
Most times I am not to blame
It's the voices in my head
it makes me feel like I am dictated
controlled by what's in the world
The whisperer will always whisper since
Shaytaan is the biggest liar
Yet don't despair
Allah will always hear His slave
The crier, the repenter
So every step I take
I know He is watching me
Tawakkul
And I know it will bring me Higher
The goal is to die as a defeater, as a trier

Growth

Oh how so much has happened
Yet Allah has carved a path
Like the men in the cave mentioned in Surah Kahf

Oh how Allah had saved me from the affairs of the Dunya
Like Yunus who was
Stuck in the stomach of a whale

Oh how so much has happened
So much calamity
Yet Allah had saved me like prophet Ibrahim in the fire

Oh, how so many onslaughts occurred
Yet Allah had raised me
Like prophet Yusuf

Lost in a well
Oh, how heartbroken I have been
But Allah had mended my little soul

By repairing it and refurbishing it with love and sincerity
Like the greatest of ALL, prophet Muhammad
May peace be upon them all

she hastened

To the believing men and women!

Wear your hijab accordingly
To the Quran and sunnah
Wear it with pride and joy

And if you want to add a touch of beauty to your eyes
Lower your gaze and decorate it with haya
And tears of repentance

If you want your nose to shine
Thank Your Rab for every breath you take
If you want to beautify your ears protect it

From listening
To what's haram and
Decorate it with what's pleasing to Allah

The Quran
If you want to add beauty to your lips
Protect the tongue from uttering haram
and decorate it with the dhikr of Allah

If you want to add beauty to your hands
Raise your hands in the supplication of your Lord
Do tasbeeh on your fingers and give charity often

If you want to add beauty to your legs
Quit going to forbidden places and decorate it with garments which
cause the legs to be unseen

If you want to add beauty to your body
wear the hijab according to Shariah and

she hastened

Maintain its purity

If you would like to add beauty to your soul
repent consistently
and keep your heart pure with dhikr

Salat-Al tawbah

Will Allah forgive me?
I push away shayaateen in my mind
As the whispers get louder

I stand up to make ablution and cleanse my skin
I prepare myself to stand before Allah
I put myself in a state of shame and hopelessness

In dire humility
For Allah to have mercy over me
I break away from the Dunya

I begin to reflect and think
Think about all that has happened
Why it had happened

I think about how my part played an operative role
in the sin
I begin to regret
And my heart tightens
as the iman acts as the source of guilt

Will Allah forgive me?
I seek refuge in Allah from the outcast of Shaytaan
I look to the left and push away Satan

I soften my heart as I rise
Regret
Regret.

Regret for this sin and the many more
But I focus on this sin alone

she hastened

I need you Allah

I need you, you hear me?
Allah is listening
My heart emerges from inside

It springs to the divine
felt during the first takbeer
I think of the sin
I focus

I focus on Allah, my Rab
I'm deeply sorry
I just want to recover

From this sheer felt guilt
I make sujood
It's going away

This burden
This heaviness
The weight

I'm becoming a bird
In the air
Through the winds

I'm shuddering in happiness
in Allah's love, mercy and warmth
Oh Allah, please don't lead me astray
I beg you Oh Allah
take me out of this darkness
And fold me into your light

she hastened

Ya Ummati

Woe to you;
did you not hear the speech of Allah inviting you?
Did He not send down the revelation
the Haqq, the truth?
Ya ummati

why do you displease your Rab
when He is so close to you
Both listening and watching
But again and again
it is your Desires shown to be latching

Onto the Dunya
Ya ummati do you not fear the painful punishment that awaits
You all have individual fates
so do not associate
O ummati when you took your desires as enslavement
did you not know that your Rab is one

and To Him alone, you belong?
Had you have known that this is shirk
you'd abstain away
So afraid and regret to have been led astray
'Why had I taken Him as a friend!'

on that day you will say!
O ummati what if it was you who was being watched
By the nabi of Allah, Muhammad ﷺ when
his curtains were being drawn, and he smiled on his deathbed as he
watched his members pray Salah, his eyes twinkled

gleamed and glowed as the tears came so close

she hastened

Ya ummati
on that day He had accomplished His mission
of which Allah had bestowed upon him
O ummati had we not let Him down?

And His last words were *ya ummati* 3x,
A man unknown to you
but so close in His sacred heart for us
a chosen Man by the Lord of the worlds who had His Ummah,
me and you, so close to His heart

Ya ummati! ya ummati! ya ummati!
Wake up, death is so close
You will all be lined up
So woe to those who forgot the remembrance of their lord
And to those who are constantly remembering their Lord
Glad tidings to you whilst you are being adored

she hastened

إِنَّا لِلَّهِ وَإِنَّا إِلَيْهِ رَاجِعُونَ

'Verily we belong to Allah, and verily to Him do we return'

Qur'an 2:156

she hastened

To my beloved sisters of this ummah

You are a mother, aunt, gran, sister, Alhamdulillah
You are the believing women of this Ummah
You are one who generates the entire Ummah
It is through you where generations grow
And it in Your Womb
where a believer grows His heartbeat
So onto you is an obligation
But onto you are so many rights
So do not be upset nor be sad
When they call you oppressed
You may be wholly dressed
But it is you who are so free
from such distress
Of which the Dunya brings
You are not the one who is incurring
Cover now before you become shrewd
And in your grave
you will wear those very garments you rejected
whilst being here
And had they not told you that death is so near?
Draw upon your garments
Feel liberated, safe and protected
Free from piercing eyes of men
Free from becoming tarnished and damaged
Free from exposure and usage
Be patient upon those who mock
You are well ahead and on that day
it is those who mocked who will be in such shock
Draw upon your garments
And do not be dressed but naked
Do not be wasted
It is from you which the Ummah grows and expands

she hastened

It is from you where values are built
If it was not for you, we would be in great strife
So, o people
strive to be like that of the women of Jannah
Do not despair
Your Lord created you, He knows you more than they do
So Listen to His commands, and draw upon your garments
He knows better whilst you do not
So let them plan and plot
Know that they cannot
Overpower Your Rab, the master and king of all worlds
All praise is due to Him

she hastened

The women of Jannah

Khadijah رضي الله عنه, our mother
Wise, intelligent, gentle and influential
A wealthy and prosperous woman
'zamilooni!', He ﷺ said in trembling fear
As He heard the words of the angel Gabriel
Confused, His beloved covered Him
Provided Him with moral support

Glad tidings to Fatima رضي الله
The chosen woman to lead the women of paradise
Defended her father's noble mission
As she watched her fathers struggles
In grief and pain, she lived on

Maryam رضي الله, the only woman to have given birth
Without being touched
Pure, gentle and chaste, Her Lord had mercy on her
A righteous woman who endeared her deen
Spent her time worshipping and glorifying Allah alone

Aasiyah رضي الله, the greatest woman to live
Her faith, so unshakable
The queen who gave it up all
For the sake of her lord

she hastened

Ya Rabb, unite us with the greatest women of all, the women of Jannah.
Ameen.

Al Haya (shyness/modesty) for the sisters

Dear sisters your neck is your awrah
Dear sisters your hair is your awrah
Dear sisters your bosoms are your awrah
Dear sisters your private parts are your awrah,
Dear sisters, why do you dress, but dress naked?

Dear sisters, wearing jeans, you can't do it
Dear sisters, showing your hair, you can't do it
Dear sisters, wearing tight clothing, you can't do it
Dear sisters, beautifying the hijab, you can't do it
Dear sisters, negating the sole purpose of the Hijab, you can't do it
Dear sisters, denying the truth, you can't do it
Dear sisters, altering the hijab into modern society, you can't do it

Dear sisters, be alert of your tabarruj
Dear sisters, beware of the Fitnah
Dear sisters if you had known
what is in the mind of a man upon seeing your skin
you would not remain naked
Dear sisters, cover up before it's too
late

Dear sisters, Al haya and Iman come
hand in hand
When you see your al haya
deteriorating
It is a clear sign of your Iman
weakening

she hastened

"Haya' (modesty) and Iman (faith) are two that go together. If one is lifted, the other is also lifted."
[Recorded by al-Hakim]

"Al-Haya' is part of Iman." "Haya' does not produce but goodness."
[Recorded by al-Bukhari and Muslim]

she hastened

Fornication

The rooftop enclosed
As she dismantled with her obligations
As she forgot the remembrance of her Lord

Her iman- became blocked
corroded and broke down
Weakened was her soul

Searching for purpose, for air
Her face, dull and unlit
Her skin- impure

Had she had known
If she hadn't been so drawn into his lure
She would not be so poor

For sure
It was this that caused her to be deprived
This is why things seemed to obscure
Like a blur

The whole time
It was her
She wanted it to stop

Lost was she
Her heart was empty
shayateen, to her heart, made an entry

Enacted as her sole gatekeeper
Caused her to speak blatantly
No shame, no grace, no beauty

she hastened

Disowned her community
Her family
Her Rab

Her heart was so wounded
With disgust, with dirt, with touches
She forgot her lord so much

That it was He who was watching
That it was He who was there, so close and so near
Listening
Knowing

But ignorant was she
As she feared to be seen
Seen by the people of the Dunya
Forgotten her Lord

Lost her grace, her dignity
Her purity
Confused about her sadness
Unchaste she became

Her character lacked so much aptness
She found it difficult to be happy
And she knew what was the reason

But she kept it intact and hidden
As she continued in this sick cycle
She became trapped, no saviour

She searched for answers
She gained knowledge

she hastened

She made promises and caused the angels to deliver her messages

But she had detached from these statements
Perpetuated in these challenges
She kept it hidden

This ongoing struggle
This jihad
She kept silent and wept to her Lord
For guidance, for light
For her desires to become halted
For her practising tendencies to stop
She begged in desperation

She acquired so much knowledge
And became endeared to her Deen
She saw light ahead of her
Impure she still felt

So scared was she of the near damnation
Of yawmal Qiyammah and the restored fire
The stories of those who committed Zina (adultery/fornication)
She broke out her silence

And Her Lord saved her
She sacrificed herself
She stopped it all
Her Lord had mercy over her

As she begged for His forgiveness
She never turned back
She walks this life as one who stops the traps of Shaytan

Her Lord had saved her

she hastened

It those who repent, that Allah سُبْحَانَهُ وَتَعَالَى *favours the most*

she hastened

Hayat al Dunya (the life of this world)

Don't be worried about the Dunya
And what is in it
For no doubt, death will overtake us and it

For those who are concerned about the figure in their pockets
And how the Dunya is beautified
For those who take pleasure in the desires of this Dunya

For them is a painful regret
He will one day turn against it
So keep well away from self-conceit

As even a grain worth of pride
in the heart will not allow you to enter paradise
So do refrain away from usury and be sure to give charity
Do not let the left hand know what the right hand possesses

The soul will never find peace nor be satisfied
By worldly matters or materials
So do not become attached

Do not take so much time to beautify your home
Your wealth, your children
You will not last for so long here

The eternal abode is more enduring
More everlasting
So work for the place of eternity

Whose builder is the most merciful!
The ground, made out of pure gold
And musk it's soil; it's grass which sprouts are off saffron

she hastened

Rivers flow as pure milk and honey
And wine which flows pure in mounted streams
The birds flutter onto branches

Murmuring, glorifying Allah
Openly singing his praise
And you will say *'what misery did I face in the Dunya?*
I am sure I was not in pain'

By the vision of the gate
The sky
The land
The greenery

The scenery
You've laid your eyes on it like no other
And so entranced and mesmerised by its peace

You will forget Hayat al Dunya

she hastened

Ya Rab, Please Grant the Ummah a good Ending. Aameen.

she hastened

Al- Jannah (Paradise)

The final abode for the righteous,
And for the true mu'min (believer)
The place of Hawa and Adam ﷺ

Where they have dwelt
Where it had all began
So delightful

I wanna go
See others I have lost
Hold them so close

Tell them I missed them so much
I came in this world just passing through
And I want to travel just like Al-mu'minoon

I'm but a stranger in a hostile world and
I cannot savour this lie anymore
So hold me so close
so I may never lose the grip of the rope
I wanna go

she hastened

There was once a righteous woman

Trying to navigate through this miserable world
She sat alone on her prayer mat
released relentless tears
which streamed for hours
She lifted her hands
as if she was a beggar
as if she was a servant
as if she surrendered
she looked like she was in
total submission
she was in humility
And she whispered to her Lord
in a quiet and gentle tone, she said
'oh Allah, I know the hereafter is better for me
Please keep me going whilst I'm here
sometimes I find it difficult
to articulate the words but
I know that you are aware of what lies in my heart
I feel sick and distant to the surroundings of this Dunya
I know what I place my love in
I'm bound to receive heartbreak
because there's nothing that lasts apart from you
I need you ya rabbi. Please be pleased with me
before I depart
I'm finding it hard to cope
Make easy my task
along those who are dehumanised
and stripped to commodities. Ameen'

Soon later, to her Lord, she sobbed effortlessly in silence...

she hastened

You haven't lost everything until you've lost your Deen.
Heartfelt naseeha (sincere advice) from the unknown

CHAPTER TEN

THE EMOTIONS SERIES

she hastened

Insomnia

Sleep what?
Pillows and duvets are a mess
What not

Can't reap
Can't sleep
I just need

Somebody to speak
To hideaway my-
To retreat

Maybe discreet
What is that is sweet?
And finally, feel complete

My father

He never looks for praises
or seeks support from others
He's never one to boast
He just goes on quietly working
For those he loves the most
He has worked so hard
To be where he is at now
He has prayed so much
Loved so much
For his family to become as strong as one
His dreams are seldom spoken
His wants are very few
And most of the time his worries
Will go unspoken too
His heart so soft, so gentle and kind
He's there...a firm foundation
Through all our storms of life
A sturdy hand to hold onto
In times of stress and strife
But upholds half our genetic makeup
A model man for his daughters who he reared
His heart so full of love
O my beloved father
The greatest of blessings
My father

she hastened

The tragic sanity of life

Whose life is that? I think I know
Its owner is quite sad though
It really is a tale of woe

I watch her frown. I cry hello
She gives her life a shake
And sobs until the tears make

The other sound's the break
Of distant waves and birds awake
The life is tragic, sanity and deep

But she has promises to keep
Until then she shall not sleep
She lies in bed with ducts that weep

She rises from her bitter bed
With thoughts of sadness in her head
She idolises being dead
Facing the day with never-ending dread

Aggrieved

She gives her life a great shake
And screams
I've made a bad mistake

Life is resentful
aggrieved and deep
In her mind thoughts sink deep
They do seep

Tormented with nightmares she never sleeps
Revenge is a promise a girl should keep
She rises from her cursed bed

With thoughts of violence in her head
A flash of rage and she sees red
Without a pause, I turned and fled

she hastened

Soul sister

Dear soul sister
together we pray
day and night we say
there is going to be a better day
a day where we gain justice
dear soul sister

together we wake up in the nights, for Fajr
we cry our hearts out to Allah for Him to listen
for our sadness to disappear
for our brothers to become clear
And our pain and worries to wash away
expressed in the single tear

beloved sister do not let go
because you alone make me strong
you alone hear my heart and for the sake of Allah
I love you
my deen corrector
my deen connector
you keep me away from wrong and give me direction
hold on and together we will gain justice

promises are never broken
it will surely be fulfilled because
'surely after hardship comes ease'
and Allah will listen, surely
if not the hereafter exists
dear soul sister

if I knew it would be the last time I saw you fall asleep
I would tuck you in motionlessly

she hastened

more tightly and pray to Allah for your soul to keep
my soul sister
if I knew it would be the last time that I'd see you walk out the door
I would give you a hug
and a forehead kiss and call you back for one more

if I knew it would be the last time I hear your voice up to praise
I would record each action and word
so I can play it back on repeat to feel your senses
at times I'll make you mad, you will hate me

at times my words will wound you
but for the sake of Allah, I love you
and you will not find any other, who loves you as much as I do

she hastened

The feeling of depression

I can't breathe, this world is a sea, holding my breath down
Can't sleep, sorry
Sleep hope
Sleep desires
Sorry story

this struggle is weighing my shoulders, overburdening me
Unending tears
I see nothing, no light, no end
Why is my heart sinking so much?

Why can't I comprehend what I am feeling?
Motionless, relentless
It's so dark right now
Darkness is what I seek
dullness, numbness
I'm sick

she hastened

A cycle of repulsive emotions

Sometimes I just wish I could run away and hide
No matter where I go though, these feelings stay inside
How can I stay here and live each day a lie?
When all I want to do is close my eyes and die?

I no longer want to see the light, the light that traps me
conceals me, hurts me
The light which every day consumes me
Why does this have to go on?

I can't keep going
Just heartache and misery
And nothing and no one could correlate
I speak but inside it, it's ruefully beating- the heart is voluble

I can't keep going

she hastened

Retention. We need to escape the world, Feel the restriction
Feel the warmth
Connect
and laugh out loud until we end

she hastened

The dark side of love

A tribute to my dear friend, A

It was all a joy when we met
The instant butterflies
the argumentative days that flew by with constant sighs
I held onto my little laughs for a while
until there was a blur I noticed, this blur inflated over time

I was looking for happiness
Maybe not eternal but temporary bliss
and the 'idea' of you being a man
who took care of me and bought me roses

A man who made me feel like a spirit who was so free
But being young is not who we define as
There was a mistake-
I captured many good moments and many dark ones too

I was held as a fugitive
unable to escape because of my deep desires
and the many people who regarded us as 'goals'-
they are such mean liars

I often had to stare into the mirror
and every day there was a new insecurity
I often criticised my waist and my breasts

I always wished things were a size up
or maybe the same size as hers because it is what caught his eyes
I never considered having such thick thighs but overtime my wish list
developed and the thread was getting longer

she hastened

His eyes didn't stop piercing
at the many thighs and legs
It was never mine
My heart always pounded

I was heavy chested
there was nothing that let it weave off
I was lost in the middle of a sea
bobbing around trying to search for great help
I just wanted your attention

You made me feel so trivial
so worthless and I kept questioning whether this is really love?
If it was love, Why was all this so messed up?
You made me feel so ugly

It was like being in a domestic home
but being free when in the absence of him
I lived in this bubble of misery
A lie. But I kept going for this light-hearted imagery

Maybe I masked through April and the end of July
I got through the external smiles but I lived in torment and a dark bubble
filled with numbness
I was numb to my lust. What was love?

So here's to the man who I escaped from;
I gave you everything but it still was not enough
You made me feel like I was nothing

You belittled me and made me feel so weak
You made me believe that I would never be loved
I thought I was going wrong
But the whole time it was you, and you held me captive

she hastened

I was a fool to watch you deceive me.
I was a fool to keep on trying. I wish I let go
But I am not mad. I will not be mad

I tried so hard
And I kept going

I kept trying until it became too much to tolerate
I got in so deep that I lost who I was
I tucked in my stomach so many times

I Tried to wear certain things
just so I could be like the girl who walked down the street -
the one who you found so pleasantly attractive

You made me feel so lost and so empty
I always wished you could come back to me, Or maybe not
I just wished I could be free. I knew it was toxic

Why did you call her pretty?
Why did you watch her walk down the road?
Why did you hurt me?
I knew you were in the wrong but I couldn't help but try

I kept telling myself that it's going to be different just this time
I was battling over everything
And I just wasn't fine
I felt sick to my stomach and all alone cried
I was on a puppet show, being controlled by vulgar hardships

I was drowned in a sea full of challenges
You hurt me so much but I knew that I was numb
Something told me that it was time to let go

she hastened

This was just an illusion of love and it was drawn closer to lust
I had to let you go. I had to escape
I was ready to put you in the shadow

I was ready to rejuvenate and newly grow
Now I praise you for giving me this spiritual growth
You lost me and I lost nothing but only gained so much

I have elevated my status
These memories are now invaded into the flitting wind
So I applaud you for making me so thick-skinned

she hastened

Unforgettable emotions

I try to cut my past off, to forget and forget
but I misinterpret these hardships and challenges
I try hard enough to forget

Walk away like I'm ruined
Walk away like I'm defeated
I try to cry

But, it doesn't work
I try to conquer and hide my pain
I was not welcomed here

I was hated over there
Was different here
Affording company, closeness

In the eyes, a once-clear oceanic blue
Wavered underwater
Tears telling torrid truths

I couldn't face
Like the glowering image in the mirror
Of compensation, delusion

see myself sitting on concrete steps
That led down to the dew-laden garden
But the bite of air couldn't lift the sorrow

Rejection hurt
Wrenches deep
An emotion that we can't deny...

she hastened

The voices that circles around us
The horrors that we are terrified of
The truth is immortality

I can't lie
I have to be honest
My emotions are trying to deny

But, my actions are to be relied on
My sympathy is a shared feeling
My compassion is my affinity

Harmony and fondness is my alliance
Emotions that we can't deny are agitation
I can't shed my past off

It will be hard enough to bare
I'll forget
I will not remember
My emotions can't deny

she hastened

An Ode to the pandemic

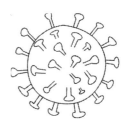

A whole long month of March in this sad plight
made their cheeks grow paler by the break of July
Lockdown from the east to the west and all in between
Freedom was certain only in dreams

The world is imploding
Falling to bits before us
Afraid of any conscious conduct
Amid this striking chaos

Shut your doors, and be close to family and friends nearby but no social
contact is permissible when you are out whether it's wet or dry
Mild symptoms? A cough, a sneeze, and there would be a fearful fright
No one is recognised due to the Corona built masks

No restaurants, no jobs, a breakdown in the economy
A breakdown in relationships
The elderly go empty-handed home
as the shelves in supermarkets lay silent and empty

And they have not excused a reason but to just keep going
a bit like the American Depression
but bigger and splendidly spread
throughout the entire nation, and all kingdoms

Sickening as these are at more risk
'weak immune systems'
to self-isolate was demanded

The coronavirus

she hastened

Elusive

I am a prisoner in my mind, thoughts and space
Fastened in my own room
I live, breathe and stay
There is no privacy, there is no space
nothing more to embrace
just memories to erase

What is love?
I have no love, ONLY hate
Reminiscing the sense from my skin
emotion and life of freedom being stripped
and ripped from my hands as I cry out for it to stay

Sometimes it just gets too much
and I feel that I've lost touch
I'm aware that the road is long
but there is nothing that could make me strong
Misery is where I belong

I was too late, I begged for mercy but it was too late
I'll never get to lay in the arms of freedom again
I pray that those who are secluded and are in a state of isolation to be
provided with freedom and mystery abstains

Ameen

CHAPTER ELEVEN

THE SPIRITUAL SERIES

A conversation between me and Allah #1

Allah: o my slave!

Slave: I was thinking of you.

Allah: *smiles* Why do you cry?

Slave: I look back at what I was and there's a flood streaming and becoming an ocean over me.

Allah: but didn't I tell you, I will take care of your affairs? Why do you worry?

Slave: I feel a deep surge of emotion in my heart. Ya Allah, please enslave me.

Allah: wipe away those tears my beautiful slave, come back to me, my arms are opened for you. Bring your broken pieces with you, I will repair them for you. I am waiting.

Slave: *wipes tears* you will grant me your forgiveness?

Allah: had they not told you, I am the most merciful, the most gracious?

Slave: *sobs effortlessly*

she hastened

Allah had reminded me; a conversation between me and Allah #2

Slave: But isn't it what's in my heart which matters? He will read my heart and understand.

Allah: No my slave, I want your inner beauty to be portrayed outwardly so the kuffar (disbelievers) do not excel and you do not become a subject to them nor a matter of imitation. This is for the greater good.

Slave: But I am improving, I am young, young in my spirits and my body.

Allah: But didn't I remind you of death in such a profound way? Had I not made it clear that I swear by the night and dawn, your life will pass! There is no time. There is no date. Seconds are remaining!

Slave: But my mother nor my father has gotten to their time yet, nor do I feel frail in my bones and my blood is energised. I will enjoy this world first.

Allah: But hadn't you read up on the verse I have revealed upon my messenger? This life is nothing but a fleeting place and decievement. Everything will be destroyed when I shall command it to! Everything shall perish! Nothing will live! Only I will last! You shall return to Me! And I make a promise to you that the time is near! Do you not see the signs my slave?

she hastened

Qun Faya Qun

(Quran 36:82)

Our mighty plans and His little 'Qun'

Do not despair

she hastened

My one sujood

Once upon a serene night
She gazed upon the beaming light
Which the moon had created
She gazed upon the sky and felt such comfort

She cleansed her skin with drops of water
Purified herself from top to bottom
And glorified her lord
Showed gratitude to Him

She laid down her blue prayer mat
And was ready to surrender
To her Lord
Her King

To the lord of the worlds
She left everything behind
As she raised her hands for the first takbeer
Her Lord had heard her praise

And commanded upon the angels to drop a wall between
Herself and the Dunya
For Himself and His slave to be alone
To communicate

And she knelt
This night
For a little longer
She wept as she buried deep in sujood

To wash away

she hastened

To dust of all materialism
She had secluded in total submission
She began to whisper and whimper

Her soul was shuddering in fear, as she felt so close
As she was in such humility
She declared Him as one
Begged for his forgiveness

'Ya rab grant me your forgiveness'
She sobbed into the darkness as her eyes shut in this position
She wept and wept and wept
Uttered no words
But her lord knew

What distress the heart was in
and what rest it needed

she hastened

God's unending mercy

And when it gets hard our tears get stuck in our throat because we are unable to speak but Allah understands every shape of our tears, and we forget our purpose and our way of life. we are here temporarily and next, we are gone eternally

And every hardship is caused by him so we forget to say Alhamdulillah because we forsake his plan. And he promises us nothing but happiness and peace for he is ever merciful so that's why he asks us to have patience, and surely this world is merely a test

So we have to keep compelling and stand up to our challenges to be blessed. Because Allah doesn't give a hardship that is beyond our ability it's designed to fit our ways and needs. It's there to test us but most importantly to bless us!

she hastened

Praying

I'm crying
But no one can hear me
I'm silent

I prostrate to Allah in darkness
I'm in a battle, waiting to defeat this challenge
I get drowned in difficulties, in hardships

And my heart aches and pains from the mental misery
I wish I could find some sort of Liberty
I'm being consumed from night till dawn

But my hands never stop opening to conform
My tears fall and I feel the damage through my skin as they soak in
I hear the drops and small weeps in my heart
as I toss and turn I become a burden to the darkness

I mask my day with no clue or awareness
I get questioned on my motive
but I'm merely just vulnerable and sufferable

she hastened

And to the waves that destroyed me, I surrender to you for making me the person I am today. So strong. So bold. So capable.

she hastened

4.15 AM; thoughts

Ya Rab, I know you hear me. I can't speak but my tears speak. You know every reason behind every drop. My hope, I have no one but you. Grant me my needs engraved within my heart and fulfil them for me. Make it easy for me. Ameen.

We were two strangers as we grew. But our souls were meant to be. It is Allah who always knew.

she hastened

And when the light beams upon me wherein there's darkness around. I ask
Allah to extend your life and to let it not be this day. Ameen.

she hastened

And if Allah took the life out of your heart right now. My soul would be elsewhere in another universe. Lost I would be. Yearning for the light that will again lead me to you.

she hastened

I may be silent. But my silence is what you can read through my mind when it's enclosed and sealed. And together the two hearts beat and when one stops, the other one stutters.

she hastened

My trip to Mecca; Saudi Arabia

The land of revelation
My heart was quivering
The very floor upon which
my prophets (peace and blessings upon them all)
have walked on

This air, so light and tranquil
So much peace upon just entering the city
My heart is so much at rest
What misery had I been in?
I had forgotten

We hurried to our hotel room
To become in a state of ihram
We walked our way to the prominent destination
Upon where the beauty laid
Upon which was constructed by my prophet Ibrahim and Ismail
(peace and blessings be upon them) 1600 years ago

As my eyes fixated onto the crowded monument
My eyes watered
They were blurred
My heart was both trembling
and shuddering in overwhelming peace

Allah, my merciful Lord, had invited me and my family to His home
To supplicate to Him
To glorify Him
To complete our umrah for the very first time

Completeness felt in my bones
I was at his service

she hastened

My iman rose to the call of Allah
As I heard the adhan

she hastened

CHAPTER TWELVE

THE HOME SERIES

she hastened

To my beloved sister

I want to sit in Jannah
in the valley of trees and gardens of flowers and tell you
Tell you that we have finally made it
It is Jannah where I want to sit with you
and cry out of happiness that the pain was worth every bit

she hastened

You need to hear it

Why do you fret over your body;
when what your Lord had given you is so beautiful and free
You masked it so much
But I see it so clearly

Why do you shed those tears?
When you know it will end
When you know that everyone will leave
But remaining will Be Allah

Your closest friend
So dear soul sister
You could shed the tears
Feel the knot in your throat

But not a day goes by
where your Lord does not think of you
Watching over you
Protecting you

I know our hearts have been filled with terror
Our minds bewildered and invaded with thoughts
Thoughts that have brought fear
But dear soul sister, hadn't I told you that to me you are so dear

And it is so clear
That not one day goes passing by
when you are not in my duas
I want to tell you how it would be
If you were to leave, how hard it would be

If only you could see what distress my heart would be

she hastened

I would only dream
Of paradise to come
So that I could run to you

Tell you how much I had missed you
Tell you that you didn't have to worry
About those times you covered up
Excessively

Those times you had shed those tears in silence
Know that I understand
Know that this fear will end
So why do you cry?

she hastened

Home

Home
A sweet, safe and secure destination
Right?

Home. A place of worship
a place of safety
Like the womb of a mother

Home

Faltered at the moment
Patiently seeking guidance
In secrecy

unending fear as to what shall occur next
A movement is made
The hands began to twitch and shake

Overhead there was a solitude group
Hurdled, like sheep
When will it be over?

And the sounds of destruction begin to grow
expand and hurt the ears
Terror-stricken

Disseminate this awareness
No one had known
What had gone on at home

All alone, In bed so cold
Everything remains untold

she hastened

Go ahead and take this word

And please tell the world!
If you had known
Your soul would be stoned

Her Lord knew she would pull through
So He chose her as the one
To go through this mayhem

Repulsive emotions
Disgust and fear
Don't pity her, just

Go tell the world!

she hastened

Just forget

I'm going to sit here
Light up some candles
Put my feet up

Forget what went on yesterday
Flowers in my vase
Centre, on the counter

Messy hair
Grab a drink before I wash away
All the grub leftover from yesterday

Like it didn't happen
Maybe get rid of the eye bags today
I'm going to

Tie my hair back
Maybe some heatless curls
Put on my wedding dress
Dance around
And just forget

she hastened

Lost

My wounds speak
Mouth sealed
They do cut deep
and infatuate my mind

I'm loose
Heartbreak was impending
No direction

Sanity I need
Where do I go
Trying to take things slow

Maybe it'll get better
But for how long will this wait occur?
For how long will I tremble in so much fear?

Meaning of life

Little kindnesses enjoy

Intolerable cruelties feel

Former woes flame

Emotional pitfalls eff

she hastened

Fear

Terror, destruction and adversity!
He is gone
We are happy

But afraid
So we must hide
He never did see this side

We are eating
But are not enjoying
When will he arrive?

Is on our minds
The sound of a car locking from outside
We drop our plates and get into position

To our hiding spots
I'm behind a door
Curled up, vulnerable

She's in the bathroom
In the bathtub
Playing dead

Now we await
For his arrival
We are safe, in our positions

What comes next
Is not in our safety net
But we are close to safety

she hastened

That's all that had mattered
Just a few minutes of laughter whilst he was gone
Forgetting the misery we relive every day

Laughing out so loud whilst he was away
Or else we could not mutter
Or Utter such sounds

Hushing and shushing in silence
Vigilant over the words we use
As it may strike violence
Or destructive abuse

Unending fear everywhere
Disclosed and in such seeming secrecy
Fear of mind, fear of actions, fear in the air
living, breathing, smelling, fear everywhere

Difficulty in sleeping
Sleep trapped
Sleep escapism
We awoke to burnt notes
Cash and coins all scattered around
All of which were snatched away
Aggressively, the day that had passed by

she hastened

laying on my beating chest with great triumph and grief she said
'This is not normal'
And her eyes watered.
Mohima

she hastened

I'm sorry

I'm sorry you had to go through all of this
I wish I could give you back your youth
When you were so beautiful

Your body so energised
So curved and so thick-skinned
I'm sorry you lost your skin

I'm sorry you lost your hair
I'm sorry your hands are stained so much with burnt marks
I'm sorry you lost your teeth before old age came to you
I'm sorry for playing my part in stressing you out

I'm sorry you lost your clothing
as you sacrificed everything you had overtime
I'm sorry you became deprived of your health, your wealth, your youth
I'm sorry you lost so much
I'm sorry that you had to go through all this terror

Which you did not deserve
I'm sorry for your heart that struck fires
I'm sorry for the mistakes people made against you
For the lies, they said against you

For the rumours, they spread about you
For the many people who expressed hate towards you
I'm sorry that you could not feel beautiful when you wanted to
I'm sorry that your youth was snatched away
And every time I watch your transition

On those captured photographs
I wish I could halt everything for you

she hastened

I'm sorry for everything when all you wanted was for us to be happy
I'm sorry for the nights that you shed your tears
For the nights you prayed, to God to take your life away
I'm sorry for the days I had to hear you weep so loud

as your heart was torn and was in so much pain
I'm sorry I had to bring you that glass of water
As if a glass of water would make everything okay

And to those days I always made the same promise every day
That someday, one day
I'll make it up to you
I'll never stop making you smile, laugh and cry in happiness

I'm sorry that it still affects you today
That your body and soul has weakened
I'm sorry that you are exhausted
I'm sorry that you lost yourself in this tragic process

Of building your own family
I'm sorry that it didn't work out for you
I'm sorry that you couldn't breathe on that disordered night
That very day

I'm sorry

she hastened

If paradise lies under your feet, paradise awaits for you,

You'll forget every pain you were dipped in, here in this Dunya.

she hastened

10:30 PM; The result of being a gang member

We had received a phone call
A scream had followed
Soon later we had evacuated outside into the darkness
In the garden

Feared for our lives
Praying in silence
They were after us
Threats, slurs, and bigotry
Blackmail

No one knew
Barefoot we hid in silence
Before they had raided our home
Before they got to us

Silence we were, hushing around
Not talking
They carried weapons
In grave danger, we were all

Prayers muddled up in so much fear
Hands shaking
Heartbreaking

she hastened

Molested

Peacefully she slept
Sound and in her chamber
Her privacy, her comfort
Windows shut
She's barely clothed

He made an entrance
Very quietly
His skilful footsteps making its way
To her adorning sweet sleep

His breath quiet
So immersed onto her laying body
She turned around
Upon hearing noises of shuffling

She felt a soft graze on her ankle
A continuous stroke
Making its way up to her body
She opened her eyes in the darkness

And she saw, it had been him
Silenced was she
Her heart voluble
Unable to speak
Confused was she

Pretending to sleep
She shuffled her feet in strife
To try and defeat
But pressed down he

she hastened

Onto her untouched body
So confused was she
The strokes intensified
Broke into her like she was free

She sobbed so effortlessly
So close was he
His hands, his body,
And so silence was she

Caressed she was to become
Robbed off her ethereal body
Upon her entire body
Not an inch now left untouched
Her heart raced
Quiet was she

silence was she
With streaming quiet tears
So confused she had been
Her garments being removed

His actions maximised
'Move' finally said she- but
Deaf was he, as he pressed down her little body
Upon her shoulders was his weight
Pressed down with his hands

silence was she
As she wept into the darkness
For how long would this be?

she hastened

The wound is the place where the light enters you.
Rumi

she hastened

The peacemaker

'Worry less,
This is life is full of tests'

My flesh. My blood

The weak can never forgive
Forgiveness is the attribute of the strong
Mahatma Gandhi

she hastened

The soul has been given its own ears to hear things minds does not understand
Rumi

she hastened

About the author

Samreen believes divinity and spirituality is the way to break through the storms of hardships and oppression in any walk in life. Her writings have mastered the impression in those that are dear to her. It is through words she expresses her grievances and it is words alone who enact as an ear to listen to her woes. Her name, 'samreen' was kept by her father. The quranic meaning of the name 'samreen' is one that is 'beneficial' and 'fruitful/plentiful', suggesting that she is valuable and is constructive for others, for situations and the world. She believes she has obligations to uphold, values to embellish and spread goodness upon everyone, that of which is beneficial. Samreen acknowledges the little things and the hidden feelings which are embedded and never spoken about. The miseries which are veiled in one's ego are dwelt upon through her strategic expressions. She believes she has a duty on this earth, a duty to make a positive impact.

Her favourite animal is birds of all species, she views birds as the embodiment and epitome of freedom and power. The wings which spread in the sky and the mystic murmurs they spread around the earth is uniquely mysterious to her. Samreen strives to be like the spirit of a bird, to fly so high, to spread her wings in liberty and forget the world through the imminent clouds.

she hastened

To birds belong the entire earth as their home. So freely moved without the need to grasp the air or clouds. Powerful.

she hastened

Printed in Great Britain
by Amazon